Tulips

This book has been reviewed
for accuracy by
Jerry Doll
Professor of Agronomy
University of Wisconsin—Madison.

Library of Congress Cataloging in Publication Data

Pohl, Kathleen.
  Tulips.

  (Nature close-ups)
  Adaptation of: Chūrippu / Hidetomo Oda.
  Summary: Text and photographs examine the life
cycle of tulips.
  1. Tulips—Juvenile literature. [1. Tulips]
I. Oda, Hidetomo. Chūrippu. II. Title. III. Series.
QK495.L72P64   1986   584'.324   86-26238

ISBN 0-8172-2709-1 (lib. bdg.)
ISBN 0-8172-2727-X (softcover)

This edition first published in 1987 by Raintree Publishers Inc.

Text copyright © 1987 by Raintree Publishers Inc., translated by
Lora Sharnoff from *Tulips* copyright © 1980 by Hidetomo Oda.

Photographs copyright © 1980 by Hidekazu Kubo.

World English translation rights for *Color Photo Books on Nature*
arranged with Kaisei-Sha through Japan Foreign-Rights Center.

1 2 3 4 5 6 7 8 9 0   90 89 88 87 86

Tulips

Adapted by
Kathleen Pohl

Raintree Publishers

Milwaukee

◀ **Tulips blooming in spring-time.**

Tulip flower stalks grow straight up, sometimes as high as two feet. The flower blooms at the tip of the stalk. Usually, just a single flower blooms on the plant.

▶ **Close-up of a tulip flower.**

Flowers are the reproductive parts of the plant, from which seeds form. The tulip flower has one female pistil surrounded by six male stamens. At the tip of the stamens are the anthers (arrow) which contain the male pollen grains.

Tulips are one of the surest signs of spring. Along with crocuses and daffodils, they are one of the earliest flowers to bloom after the winter snow melts. These lovely, graceful flowers come in many colors—reds, yellows, whites, pinks, and purples. The popular garden flowers are now very common, but there once was a time when tulips were highly prized and very scarce.

Tulips originated in Turkey. The word *tulip* comes from a Turkish word meaning "turban."

In the 1500s, tulips were introduced to Europe. They became very popular, especially in the Netherlands. Tulip bulbs were not plentiful at first, and it took many years to grow a flower from a tulip seed. So tulips became a symbol of wealth and status. Soon a craze called "tulipomania" spread across Holland. Sometimes a single bulb sold for as much as $10,000. People lost whole fortunes buying and selling tulip bulbs. Finally, the Dutch government began to regulate the buying and selling of the bulbs to keep the country from going bankrupt. Today, tulips are still highly valued in Holland. More tulips are grown there commercially than in any other country of the world.

▼ Tulip bulbs. Some tulip bulbs are too small to produce flowering plants the first year. Those bulbs that measure an inch or more in diameter are the most likely to produce plants with blooms.

▲ **Cross-section of a tulip bulb.**

A brown skin, called the cuticle, covers the bulb. The scales make up the bulk of the bulb's interior.

▲ **The bud and scales removed from a bulb.**

The fleshy white leaves that surround the bud contain stored nutrients.

Tulip plants are able to live year after year because they form bulbs beneath the ground. Each bulb contains a bud from which the root, stem, leaves, and blossoms of a new plant can form. The bud is enclosed in layers of fleshy white leaves, or scales, that contain stored nutrients. They provide nourishment for the bud as it sprouts, or germinates, and goes through its early period of growth.

Tulips planted from bulbs grow much faster than those planted from seeds. That is beccause the bulb's large supply of stored nutrients gives the plant such a headstart in its development.

▶ **The lily family.**

Tulips belong to the lily family. The scientific name for the family is Liliaceae. Crocuses and lilies belong to the same family. They are also grown from bulbs.

crocuses

gold-banded lilies

◀ Tulips are one of the earliest garden flowers to bloom in the spring.

In the United States, the snow is usually gone before tulips emerge in the spring. But sometimes they may poke up through a late season snow.

▶ A tulip plant beginning to unfold its leaves.

The tulip plant grows long, broad, pointed leaves. They unfurl as they push through the soil.

Tulip bulbs should be planted in autumn, before the ground freezes. Bulbs are usually planted four to six inches deep. They grow best in well drained soil.

The bulbs begin to sprout almost immediately. Roots form from the sprouts at the base of the bulb. They reach out into the soil, anchoring the plant and taking in water and nutrients. While the bulb itself seems to be resting in the cold ground through the winter, much activity is actually going on inside it. The bud begins to develop the leaves and stem of the new plant. Male and female flower parts begin to form. Six male stamens develop around the thick, tube-like female pistil.

In spring, as the snow begins to melt and the air temperature rises, the tulip plant begins to push its way up through the ground.

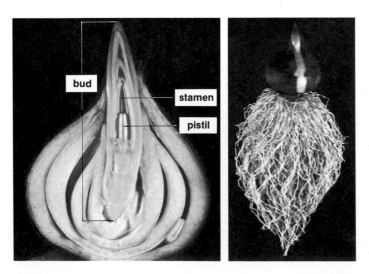

bud

stamen

pistil

◀ Cross-section of a bulb (left photo) and its roots (right photo) during germination.

Inside the bulb, the leaves, stem, and flower parts of the new plant begin to form. The roots grow in a complex network as they reach out into the soil.

◀ **A field of tulip plants.**

As large, green leaves develop on the tulip plant, they capture the sun's energy and produce food for the plant. The plants need lots of nourishment so that flower stalks can form and flowers can bloom.

▶ **Early-flowering tulips.**

This variety of early-flowering tulips starts blooming in March. The flower stalks are very short.

The tulip plant develops thick, sturdy, pointed green leaves as it grows. The leaves are very important because they produce food for the growing plant. The complex process by which green plants make food is called photosynthesis. Photosynthesis means "to produce with light." It is the tulip plant's green leaves that capture the sun's energy and combine it with carbon dioxide and water to produce food for the growing plant.

▶ **A sprout developing from a bulblet (left photo) and the leaf of a bulblet growing aboveground (right photo).**

Often, smaller bulblets form from the parent bulb. They are capable of producing new plants.

◀ A flower bud appearing.

Once the long tulip leaves unfold, the flower bud comes into view. It is small and green and hard at first.

▶ A flower bud starting to mature.

The small green bud swells up and changes color as it matures. The flower stalk which supports the bud grows taller.

As the long, pointed tulip leaves unfold, the flower bud that was hidden inside them becomes visible. Each tulip plant has only one flower stalk and, usually, only one flower bud. The small green bud swells up as the flower gets ready to open.

By the time the tulip is ready to bloom, all of the stored nutrients in the bulb have been used up. The leaves have taken over the job of supplying the plant with food.

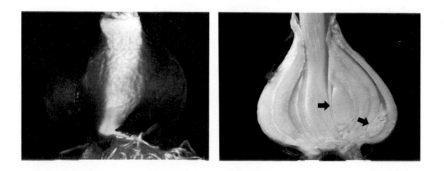

◀ A bulb whose nutrients have been used up (left photo) and a cross-section of the bulb (right photo).

Once the bulb's nutrients have been used up, the cuticle cracks open. Inside, tiny bulblets have formed which can produce new plants.

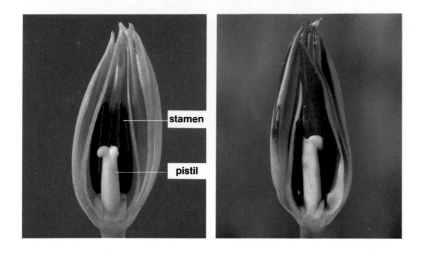

stamen

pistil

◄ **The development of a tulip bud.**

The young bud is still green and its stamens and pistil are not yet mature (left photo). As the stamens and pistil mature, the petals begin to take on color (right photo).

► **A field of tulips in bloom.**

As the stamens and pistil mature in the bud, it grows larger. The color of the bud changes and soon the flower "petals" are ready to open. The tulip "petals" are actually both petals and sepals. Sepals are the green, leafy structures that enclose and protect the flower bud on many plants. As the bud opens, the sepals fold back, and the bright flower petals come into view. It is easy to tell the sepals and petals apart on such plants. But in tulips, the sepals and petals look alike and are generally just called petals.

Often, in early spring, a tulip will start to bloom and then will close back up if the weather turns cold or rainy. But when the sun comes out, the tulip flowers will open again.

● **A tulip flower opening.**   Once the bud takes on color, the flower petals gradually open up.

◀ **A field of tulips in bloom.**

These tulips were raised in a part of Japan where the sandy soil is very similar to that in the Netherlands.

▶ **Lovely tulips swaying in the breeze.**

Tulips open and close their petals in response to changes in the temperature of the air. On cold, rainy days, the petals remain closed to protect the pistil and stamens.

Many varieties of tulips are grown throughout the world. In Holland, tulip growers raise almost 2,000 different kinds. Tulips come in a rainbow of colors, and in different sizes and shapes. The most common tulip flower is cup-shaped or bell-shaped.

Tulips are grown in flowerbeds in parks and gardens to give pleasure to people passing by. Florists sell great numbers of the cut flowers, especially around Easter time. And tulip plants are often raised by growers for the bulbs they produce. The bulbs are sold in stores in the fall to people who want tulips to bloom in their gardens in the spring.

In addition to giving pleasure to people everywhere, the beautiful tulip flowers serve another purpose. The brightly colored petals attract insects. Insects help a process called pollination to take place. Without pollination, most kinds of plants are not able to produce seeds, from which new plants can grow.

● **Unusual varieties of tulips.**

Triumphator

Fringed Beauty

West Point

Alladin

17

▼ A close-up view of the pistil and stamens inside a tulip flower.

The thick green tube in the middle of the stamens is the pistil. Its yellow tip is the stigma. The tulip's anthers may be covered with yellow or purple pollen.

▲ **A tulip losing its petals.**

The tulip petals are thick and sturdy and last quite a while. They fade in color eventually and fall off one by one.

The pistil and stamens are the reproductive parts of the plant; they make it possible for new seeds to form. They are enclosed in the tulip's brightly colored petals.

The pistil is a thick green tube. Its sticky tip is called the stigma. The pistil is surrounded by the stamens. The tips of the stamens, the anthers, contain the male pollen grains.

▲ **This pistil remains after the petals have fallen.**

The petals and some of the stamens have fallen from this plant. If the stigma was pollinated, seeds will soon begin to grow inside the pistil.

In order for pollination to take place, a pollen grain from an anther must land on the stigma. Insects often help this to happen as they flit from flower to flower, searching for food. Tulips and other flowers produce pollen and nectar which butterflies, bees, and other insects like to eat.

● **How a tulip is pollinated.**

When the pollen from an anther touches the stigma of a pistil, pollination has taken place. New varieties of tulips are formed when pollen from one kind of tulip touches the stigma of another kind of tulip.

The stigma is shaped like a triangle.

A stigma covered with pollen.

▲ A tulip fruit growing larger.　　　　　▲ A mature tulip fruit starting to dry up.

Once the pollen touches the stigma, it begins to swell up. Soon, it sends a long tube down the pistil to the ovary, where female egg cells are located. Sperm cells are released from the pollen and join with the eggs, fertilizing them. From these fertilized eggs, seeds begin to grow.

Meanwhile, the flower petals drop from the plant, one by one. The pollen grains are scattered by insects and the wind. The stamens, too, begin to fall from the plant. Soon, all that remains at the top of the tulip stalk is the thick green pistil. Rows of tiny seeds are forming inside its protective walls. The pistil swells up as the seeds grow larger. When it has ripened, the ovary, now called a fruit, may measure more than two inches long and almost an inch in diameter.

Once the fruit has matured, it begins to wither and dry up, forming the seed pod. Eventually, it will crack open, and many thin, tiny seeds will spill from it.

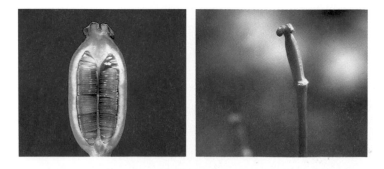

◀ The development of the tulip fruit.

A pollinated pistil develops into a fruit and bears seeds (left photo). A pistil which has not been pollinated will dry up without forming a fruit (right photo).

▼ Tulip seeds that have spilled out from a seed pod.

The tulip seeds are thin and dry and can easily be scattered by the wind. About 200-300 seeds are packed inside a single fruit.

◀ **Tulip seeds that have started to sprout.**

The sprout becomes the root of the new plant.

▶ **A seed leaf pushing its way out of the ground.**

The seed leaf is called that because it actually forms inside the seed coat. Many kinds of plants have two seed leaves. They are called dicots. Plants like tulips and lilies that have only one seed leaf are called monocots.

Each tiny tulip seed has stored nutrients and embryonic material from which a new plant can form. But it is very difficult and takes a very long time to grow a flowering tulip plant from a seed.

If a seed is planted in the fall, it will remain inactive, or dormant, during the winter. In the spring, if growing conditions are right, the tiny seed will begin to sprout. The sprout forms the root of the new plant. Soon a single seed leaf, with the seed coat still attached to its tip, will push its way through the soil. During the first year, the seed leaf may grow about four inches high. No new leaves or flowers will form on the seedling plant. Eventually, the seed leaf dies, leaving a tiny bulb that has formed in the earth.

◀ **Tulip seed leaves growing in a flower pot.**

The seed coats are no longer attached to these seed leaves. The tallest seed leaf here is about four inches high.

▶ **Tulip bulbs in their first year (arrow) and a regular bulb.**

The bulbs that formed from seedling plants are only about as large as a match head. Bulblets that form from parent bulbs may be an inch or more in diameter.

| A tulip in its second year | In its third year | In its fourth year | In its fifth year |

▲ **The development of a tulip grown from a seed.**

With yearly replantings, a tulip bulb grown from a seed will gradually grow big enough to produce a flowering plant.

A tulip bulb grown from a seedling will not produce a flowering plant the year after it was first planted, or the year after that. Instead, each year it will produce only one slender leaf above the ground. But each autumn, the tulip bulb will grow a bit larger. Finally, five years after the seed was planted, the tulip bulb will have grown large enough to produce a flowering plant. So it is easy to understand why most people plant tulips from bulbs, rather than from seeds.

Tulip plants grown from bulbs produce flowers that look like those of the parent plant. But tulips grown from seeds inherit traits, or characteristics, from each parent plant. That is how new varieties of tulips are developed. And that is the main reason why some growers plant tulips from seeds.

first year   second year   third year   fourth year   fifth year

◄ **A bulb raised from a seed.**

The bulb grows from the size of a match head in its first year to a size large enough to produce a flowering plant in its fifth year.

▼ **Thousands of the same kind of tulips growing in a field.**

Tulips that are grown from seeds inherit characteristics from each parent plant. Two different kinds of tulips are often crossed, or interbred, to develop new varieties. But that takes many years because it takes so long to grow tulips from seeds.

◀ **Two women picking tulip flowers.**

The flowers are removed from the top of the tulip stalk before seed pods have begun to form.

▶ **Tulip flowers being thrown away in a rice paddy field in Japan.**

These tulips that are picked cannot be used as cut flowers because only the flowers are plucked off. The stalk and leaves are left on the plant so nourishment can be provided for the bulblets.

People who raise crops of tulips for their bulbs must pick the tulip flowers as soon as they bloom. This prevents the growth of seeds and fruits. When a plant is forming seeds, it sends almost all its nutrients to the ovary, where the seeds are developing. But if seeds are kept from forming, the plant is able to store the extra food it is producing.

The tulip stem carries the nutrients down to the bulblets that are forming in the parent bulb. As extra food is stored in the bulbs, they grow larger and healthier. The plant's new bulbs do most of their growing in this period after flowering. The longer the tulip plants stay green, the larger the bulbs are likely to be.

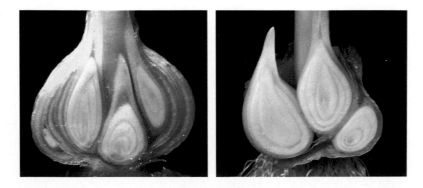

◀ **A bulb developing during the flowering period.**

The left photo shows the bulb of a tulip plant about to flower. The right photo shows how large the bulblets have grown since the flower was picked.

▲ A tulip leaf that has begun to wither.

▲ A leaf which has completely withered up.

By midsummer, the leaves and stalk of the tulip plant have withered and turned brown. The last of the plant's nutrients have been stored in the bulbs hidden in the ground. It is time to dig up the tulip bulbs.

If the tulip plant was a healthy one, several good-sized bulbs should have formed in a cluster. Each bulb is protected by a brown skin, called the cuticle. The cuticle is actually made up of the outer scales of the bulb which have used up their supply of water and stored nutrients. The cuticle has substances in it which help to prevent diseases and keep mold from forming on the bulbs.

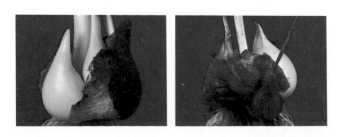

◄ Newly formed bulbs.

The bulbs in the left photo are at their peak, and were dug from the ground just before the plant's leaves started to wither. The bulbs in the right photo were dug up a few weeks later. Brown cuticles have started to form on the bulbs.

▼ **Tulip bulbs grown in a flower pot.** Several bulbs are clustered together on this withered tulip stalk. The arrow shows the dried-up scales of the parent bulb.

◀ **Tulip bulbs in a storehouse.**

People who grow large crops of tulips put the bulbs in storehouses once they have been harvested. This helps keep them dry until fall. The warm temperatures of summer help the bulbs to mature, but too much rain can cause mold and mildew.

▶ **Tulips with yellow flowers.**

When bulbs from these tulips are planted in the fall, bright yellow tulips will flower from them in the spring.

Once the bulbs have been dug up, they should be aired and dried out for a few weeks. Then they can be cleaned and sorted according to size. Any bulb that measures an inch or more in diameter is likely to produce a flowering tulip the following spring.

The bulbs should be replanted in September or early October, before the first frost. Many of them will take root almost as soon as they are planted. The embryonic material that will form the bud of the new plant develops through the winter. The growing bud is nourished by the stored food in the scales of the bulb. In spring, the green leaves of new tulip plants will push their way up through the soil.

● **Development of a tulip bulb.**

The scales are packed tightly together in a bulb that has just been dug up.

The scales contain stored nutrients. A tiny plant embryo begins to form in the center of the scales.

The embryo forms the bud of the new plant. Leaves, stem, and flowers will grow from it.

GLOSSARY

bulb—an underground storage organ for tulips and some other kinds of plants, containing stored food and a bud from which a new plant can form. (pp. 5, 7, 8)

bulblets—small bulbs that form inside the parent bulb, capable of producing new plants. (pp. 11, 26)

cuticle—the brown, outer layer of scales that forms a skin over the tulip bulb, helping to protect it from mold and disease. (pp. 7, 28)

fruit—the ripened ovary of a plant, including its seeds. (pp. 20, 26)

monocots—plants that have just one seed leaf, or cotyledon. (p. 22)

photosynthesis—the complex process by which green plants make food, with the help of chlorophyll, a substance found in the plants' leaves, and energy from sunlight. (p. 11)

pollination—the process in which pollen is transferred from an anther to the tip, or stigma, of a pistil. (pp. 16, 19)

scales—the thick, fleshy leaves of the tulip bulb which contain stored nutrients and help to protect the plant bud. (pp. 7, 28)

sepals—the green, leaflike structures that enclose and protect the flower buds on many plants. (p. 14)